Chakras & Mudras for Beginners

Mudras for Balancing and Awakening Chakras —the Powerful Personalized Meditation Guide, Cleanse and Activate Your 7 Chakras, Feel Energized

Written by
Mia Rose & Priya Sareeh

©Copyright 2019 by Mia Rose - All rights reserved.

This document is geared towards providing exact and reliable information in regards to the topic and issue covered. The publication is sold with the idea that the publisher is not required to render accounting, officially permitted, or otherwise, qualified services. If advice is necessary, legal or professional, a practiced individual in the profession should be ordered.

From a Declaration of Principles which was accepted and approved equally by a Committee of the American Bar Association and a Committee of Publishers and Associations.

In no way is it legal to reproduce, duplicate, or transmit any part of this document in either electronic means or in printed format. Recording of this publication is strictly prohibited and any storage of this document is not allowed unless with written permission from the publisher. All rights reserved.

The information provided herein is stated to be truthful and consistent, in that any liability, in terms of inattention or otherwise, by any usage or abuse of any policies, processes, or directions contained within is the solitary and utter responsibility of the recipient reader. Under no circumstances will any legal responsibility or blame be held against the publisher for any reparation, damages, or monetary loss due to the information herein, either directly or indirectly.

Respective authors own all copyrights not held by the publisher.

The information herein is offered for informational purposes solely, and is universal as so. The presentation of the information is without contract or any type of guarantee assurance.

The trademarks that are used are without any consent, and the publication of the trademark is without permission or backing by the trademark owner. All trademarks and brands within this book are for clarifying purposes only and are the owned by the owners themselves, not affiliated with this document.

Contents

INTRODUCTION 7

CHAPTER 1- CHAKRAS HOW THE WEST WAS WON OVER 8

CHAPTER 2- THE CHAKRAS, AN OVERVIEW 14

CHAPTER 8- THE SIXTH CHAKRA (THE THIRD EYE) 52

CHAPTER 9 THE SEVENTH CHAKRA (THE CROWN CHAKRA) 57

CONCLUSION 67

INTRODUCTION 69

CHAPTER 1- WEIGHT LOSS; A BIG PROBLEM 70

CHAPTER 2- MUDRAS TO BURN OFF EXCESS FAT 77

CHAPTER 3- DEVELOPING THE DIGESTIVE SYSTEM 81

CHAPTER 4- CURBING CRAVINGS AND BUILDING WILLPOWER 94

CONCLUSION 101

Mia Rose & Priya Sareeh

Chakras For Beginners

Understanding Chakras, Chakra Balancing & Chakra Healing, for Health & Wellness

Written By
Mia Rose

Introduction

I want to thank you and congratulate you for getting the book, "Chakras For Beginners".

This book contains proven steps and strategies on how to develop basic, essential skills to learn the art of Reiki. Taking a comprehensive look at Chakra work, the Aura and the different ways in which to train in Reiki this book covers everything you will need to know to become a Reiki practitioner.

Thanks again for reading this book, I hope you enjoy it!

- Mia Rose

Mia Rose & Priya Sareeh

Chapter 1 - Chakras How the West was Won Over

The concept of the Chakras is deeply rooted in ancient Buddhist and Hindu teaching and, for much of history, has been little known beyond these cultures. Knowledge of the Chakras gradually filtered Westward during the 1960s and 70s. In the happier, and slightly more peaceful, days when you could buy an old VW Camper van for next-to-nothing in Istanbul and set off overland for India, many young people did just that. As they returned Hippie culture exploded and in the 1960s this cultural challenge to the traditional ways of living in the west was partly developed by exposure to cultures with very different approaches to the way in which we live our lives and interact with the world around us.

The teachings of both Hinduism, and particularly Buddhism, resonated strongly with the post-war generation and this led to the popularization of some strands of Hindu practices and 'alternative' religions. They were further popularized by the celebrities of the day – notably the Beatles – but at the same time they garnered what may be considered an unfortunate reputation for being based on "New Age" Spirituality. It's important to understand that there is nothing new about either Hinduism or Buddhism. For example, Jainism, one Hindu religion, is actually one of the oldest extant religions in the world preceding by centuries Christianity and Islam and long outliving the religions of Classical Europe with which it is (at least) contemporary.

Many of the traditions found in Hinduism and Buddhism take a very different approach to our place in the universe, recognizing a link between us as individuals, our wider communities and the natural world. Hindu and Buddhist traditions see each individual as part of a much greater whole, a universal energy of which we are merely (and, at the same time, divinely) an expression. Humanity is not the only expression of this universal energy but simply a part of it. All living creatures and the planet itself are made up of, and part of, this force. Whether you are religious, or not, many of elements of these religions will strike a chord in a world in which humanity's impact on the planet seems rampantly out of control and in an age where an urgent need to re-balance our own relationship with the natural world.

Buddhists and Hindus also regard all aspects of life as linked to each other. This has led to religious, social and health practices which take a 'whole' view. Each part of our nature, our needs as humans, is seen as linked and in need of being finely balanced. The argument that our health is related to the way we live our lives is hard to dismiss, even for the more cynical or skeptical. Modern science does, in fact, make clear links between our way of life, the impact on our health and even on the wider environment. What ancient practitioners of many Eastern religions saw clearly many centuries ago is now being backed up and reaffirmed by modern science.

The Chakra system is based very much on the understanding of the universe as simply energy. It uses a simple model which aims to establish balance within our lives – in all aspects – in order to achieve a healthy body and mind. Again, understanding this doesn't need any particular religious belief. Science has long since proved that at the minutest atomic level we (and everything else) are made up simply of energy vibrating at a different frequencies. The matter that we are made of doesn't appear from nowhere when we are born nor does it disappear when we die; both energy and matter are simply in a state of constant transformation.

In this book we look at the expression of this universal energy in our own bodies and how it relates to our health, our wellbeing, our emotional and mental stability. The Chakra system is about living in harmony with yourself, the world around you and, on a deeper level, with the universe itself. You need no belief in a higher being to harness the power of Chakra healing and in this book we look at Chakras from a practical, common sense angle.

What are the Chakras?

Traditionally the Chakras are defined as centers of energy which are connected to the physical body. In total there are seven main Chakras and it's these on which this book focuses.

The Chakras are part of the energy field of our body and they are not physically visible to most people. Some practitioners who have worked with Chakras for many years are able to see clearly these energy centers and some will learn to do so as they develop a better understanding of the Chakras. Although not part of the physical body the chakras impact directly upon it and upon its correct functioning. They have a direct relation to every part of our lives and wellbeing including spiritual, mental, emotional and physical.

How to Use this Book

This book is designed to offer a practical, usable introduction to the Chakras, how they can affect our health and well being and how to identify imbalances and address these. The book is designed for those new to the concept but will also be useful for those with some experience of Chakra and energy healing. In the next chapter we take a more detailed look at what the Chakras are, and an overview of each one of the seven main Chakras. The remaining part of the book looks at each individual Chakra and how to examine the Chakra for imbalances. The final chapter provides a simple list-style section of tools that traditional (and modern) Chakra experts believe are useful in achieving balance within your Chakra energy system.

How to use this Book – For Skeptics!

A healthy dose of skepticism in life is no bad thing. For some people the concept of Chakras may seem unscientific, mystical, magical or just plain hocus-pocus. However, good skeptics don't dismiss anything without examining it at close quarters.

The Chakra system can be viewed as very real or, for the skeptical-minded, as a useful visualization and meditation tool. That our physical health is closely linked to our mental state is hard to dispute and modern science now largely agrees on this fact. Each Chakra addresses basic human functions or aspects of our nature and in doing so it focuses on creating a rounded personality, which is well grounded, strives to eat well, live well and have respect for the environment (human and natural) around us. These are fairly sensible aims in life, regardless of whether you 'believe' in Chakras or follow any other religious or ethical tradition.

In recent years physical and emotional wellbeing have been closely linked by numerous studies; stress can lead to anything from the common cold to fatal cancer or heart disease. We often feel physically ill on hearing bad news and for skeptics these simple facts and scientifically established truths are worth considering. The Chakras offer us a chance to visualize each area of our life and to make it 'real' in our minds. In doing so we can work with simple visual forms that break each area of our lives down and help us to achieve improvement.

If nothing more, the Chakras provide a mental framework in which to address our physical, emotional and spiritual needs.

In each section, consider the way in which the activities and approaches can help you to balance your emotional state and how they promote physical good health as well. Using the Chakra system doesn't require you to sign up to any religious belief system, nor does it require a great deal more than common sense to implement. Chakra healing is about healing the whole person, focusing on understanding root causes of illness, physical or mental, and on eliminating these from your life. Ultimately Chakra healing is about achieving balance in all areas of your own life and achieving harmony within the world in which you live.

Chapter 2 - The Chakras, an Overview

The word Chakra means "wheel" and the body's energy centers are described in this way because Chakras are circular, spinning energy vortexes. The purpose of these energy centers is to adjust the flow of universal energy present in the wider universe into a form that can be utilized by the human energy field. On a very simple level, imagine trying to connect a shaver directly into a plug. The resulting explosion would be damaging and not in the least harmonious! Using an adapter allows you to transform the flow of energy required for the device into the right frequencies. This, in a very simple way, is what the Chakras do for the human energy field. Regulating and modulating the energy that flows through and around us. Each Chakra spins at a different speed and is seen as a vortex, represented by a Lotus in traditional imagery. Each Chakra spins at a different rate, the lower Chakras spinning more slowly, the upper much faster. The Lotus symbol for each Chakra is seen as having a different number of petals and each is represented and visualized as a different color which has links to the purpose of the Chakras. Chakras are sometimes identified by a number (the first, second and so on) or by a name (the Root, The Sacral etc). In this book we use both the name and the number as these are common terms you'll hear when the Chakras are referred to.

Where are the Chakras Located?

The Chakra system runs along the spine; it's along the spine that the human body's main energy channel runs. This takes the form of three separate channels, one central column, running up the spine (known as the Shushumna) and two others which spiral upwards (the Ida and the Pingala) around the Shushumna. Where these two cross the Chakras are to be found. The Chakras are visualized as funnel shaped – with their narrowest points on the spine, broadening out in both directions. Each Chakra has a color and a frequency associated with it and the upper Chakra, the Crown, and the lowest, the face upwards and downwards from the Shushumna respectively while the remaining Chakras are placed horizontally.

How do the Chakras Work?

When our Chakras are in balance they allow energy to freely flow through our bodies and keep us revitalized, healthy and connected to the world around us. However, imbalances within the Chakra system can cause the energy to become blocked, leading to ill health both physical and emotional. The Chakras are like vortexes – a good analogy is to think of the water draining from a bath or sink. When the plug is free from blockages the water can drain away effectively; clogged with grime the water fails to drain, becomes stagnant and polluted. This is very much the way in which a blocked Chakra affects the energy flow within the body and why it is important to constantly maintain a healthy energy system.

The Impact of the Chakras on Our Lives

Each individual Chakra is associated with a different area of our lives. This basic principle is an important concept to understand and, whether you are a supporter of Chakra and energy healing or somewhat skeptical, examining how the Chakras relate to each area of our lives can be useful in understanding that apart from anything else the Chakra system is one based ultimately on common sense.

The First Chakra – The Root Chakra - Red

This Chakra is identified with our basic survival instinct and our feeling of grounding. It connects us to the earth and to a sense of being present in the moment.

An under-active root Chakra can lead to feelings of insecurity, nervousness, anxiety and a loss of connection with the world. Overactive, this Chakra can foster a need for control, materialism, greed and a strong aversion to change.

The Second Chakra – the Sacral Chakra – Orange

This Chakra relates to our feelings, sexuality and emotions. In a healthy balance this Chakra creates an ease of expression in emotion, without being overly emotional. Open to intimacy and expressive in relationships, along with the ability to relate to others are features that this Chakra bestows.

If the Sacral Chakra is blocked or under-active you may be distant with people, formal and find it difficult to express how you feel.

Over-active this Chakra is likely to create an over-emotional personality, often tearful and euphoric by turn. It can also affect sexuality making you overly sexual.

The Third Chakra – The Solar Plexus (or Navel) – Yellow

This Chakra is related to self-confidence and assertiveness. In balance it creates a personality which is able to stand up for itself within social groups (work or personal) and do so without being dogmatic.

Under-active the solar plexus will create indecision, low self-esteem and difficulties in asserting your needs.

Over-active this Chakra will create a domineering personality with a tendency to aggression in both their personal life and their professional.

The Fourth Chakra – The Heart Chakra – Green

This Chakra controls our emotions of love, affection and our ability to be compassionate. In balance you will be open, caring and understanding.

Under-active or blocked Heart Chakras will create a distant, cold personality which lacks empathy and compassion.

Over-active, this Chakra tends to become overbearing in relationships with others – caring too much and often pushing people away by being 'suffocating'.

The Fifth Chakra – The Throat Chakra – Blue

This Chakra, unsurprisingly, is about communication! The ability to talk, to express ideas and opinions are all covered by this energy center. Fully functioning and well balanced the Throat Chakra is also connected to self-expression in the form of creativity.

Low activity in the throat Chakra is found amongst those who are shy, very introverted and find it difficult to express themselves clearly.

Bad listeners and those who dominate in conversation or debate are likely to have a Throat Chakra which is overly active.

The Sixth Chakra – The Third Eye – Indigo

This Chakra dominates the qualities of intuition, insight and the ability to visualize. Those who are good at independent thought and action have a well-balanced sixth Chakra.

Low activity in this Chakra promotes rigidity in thinking, inability to think for yourself and reliance on others in authority (both authority figures in your life and in general).

Over-activity in this Chakra creates a personality that lives in a world of fantasy and is removed from basic realities of their own life. Severe imbalances can turn visualization into hallucination.

The Seventh Chakra – The Crown – Violet

This Chakra governs our spiritual persona and is linked closely to wisdom. It creates a sense of our place in the world and also a sense of our place as part of a wider universe.

Low activity in the Crown Chakra blocks our understanding of spirituality, making us unaware of this aspect of life.

Those with over-active Crown Chakras can ignore the other aspects of their personality, including their basic bodily needs. They spend too much time focusing on spirituality and also tend to over intellectualize issues, lacking grounding and common sense.

The Fine Tuning

As is hopefully clear from the brief description of the Chakras above, the ideal way to maintain a balanced system is for all Chakras to be operating at their optimum. The Chakra system is about balance, moderation and grounding. There is nothing magical about this, nothing esoteric. Each Chakra looks at a single area of our life and aims to balance that area but also create balance between the focus we place on each area of our lives. This is not only a key principle in the understanding of Chakras but is also the basic tenant of many modern developments in psychology and in healthy living. Excess, physical or behavioral, in any area of our life is not healthy for us and this has been recognized by those who practice Chakra Healing for many hundreds of years. Balancing our Chakra energies is about creating a wider balance in our lives and in fostering a sensible, positive attitude to *all* areas of our lives.

Holy Music and Grounded Sounds

Those familiar with yoga and meditation techniques will be aware that sound can play a significant part in both practices. Each Chakra has a sound associated with it and a different frequency associated with the Solfeggio scale. This a six tone scale that has been used in different cultures across the world, and across history, within sacred music. To Westerners the most familiar body of music in which the Solfeggio frequencies can be found is most likely to be that of Gregorian chants. However, researchers have found that these frequencies occur in many other religious traditions within chanting, meditation and choral music. The fact that from ancient times this scale has been used with sacred settings suggests that the very sounds themselves have a transformative effect – whether that be to encourage a trance-like state of meditation or release stress and relax our bodies. The Solfeggio frequencies linked to each Chakra are mentioned in the final chapter of this book, along with other tools associated with Chakra Healing.

How (and Why) Should You Balance the Chakras?

Balancing the Chakras is a very simple process and it doesn't require any great commitment of time or (necessarily) any great expense. Much has been written in recent years about the 'work-life' balance and balancing the Chakras is not so very different from attempting to achieve a healthy lifestyle that ensures you give the right priority to each part of your life. We've all seen friends or relatives focus so intently on one area of their life – be that work or family – that they burn out in some way. Some individuals may focus on a career and earning a living (and/or making a fortune). Often this results in a sudden and unexpected departure of the very family that they believed they were working for. In other cases, some individuals (often, but not always, women) focus so much on the lives of their children and/or partners that they lose sight of themselves. This in itself can push loved ones away in the process. Finding the right balance between work, family and yourself is never easy. This is very much what the Chakra system promotes – addressing every area of life that is important to each and every human and putting the 'right' amount of effort into each of these. As mentioned earlier in this book there's nothing too "new Age" about this approach to life and it's one that is recognized as beneficial by those in the medical and psychotherapy professions today.

Balancing the Chakras

To do this you need to examine your life, looking at each area that the Chakras govern. You should also do this on a regular basis to see how well-balanced your Chakras (or simply your life) are.

Examine the following areas; your contact with the natural world, time spent on your career, family and socializing time, your diet and exercise levels, your creative endeavors and self-expression, your education (formal or informal), volunteer working or simply helping others, time spent meditating or time focused on spirituality.

These basic needs all relate to the different Chakras – but they also are very simple, common and universal human needs. Under each section write down how much time you spend on each activity per day, week and month. The result will give you a clear idea of where your main priorities lie and whether one single area or group of areas dominates your life. If you focus on one or several areas at the expense of the whole this will (apart from being very normal) indicate that you need to redirect some of your energies from those sections to the others. Each area needs to have a fairly equal priority within your life and without this balance you'll find that your basic human needs are not met.

Coaxing Change

However, where you find areas that need to become more of a focus, and ones which need less, don't try to force the changes. It's important to make changes slowly over time and to allow those changes to 'embed' into your lifestyle gradually. Trying to force changes and to break old habits invariably leads to failure and disillusion. We are creatures of habit and it can take time for us to implement new ones.

If you find that you focus on work at the expense of all other areas, gradually reduce this. Take time to walk in the open air, to exercise, socialize and spend time with your family. Sign up for a basic introduction to meditation or yoga. If your life is orientated around family at the expense of everything else, consider an art class, learning a language or new skill. Importantly address each area gradually, one at a time in order to bring a new kind of balance into your life. As you do so your Chakras will also begin to re-align, to balance and function in harmony.

Mentally and emotionally this will have a big impact – a massive impact – and this will also reflect in your physical health. There is little disagreement in the medical world that happiness, mental and emotional stability all have a massive impact on our physical health. Taking this approach to balancing your Chakras and your needs is one of the most effective ways in which to create changes in both your physical and emotional health. The results can be quite astounding and they can also begin to show quickly. Increased balance, roundedness, clarity of purpose and general satisfaction in life will all stem from taking the simple steps outlined in this book.

Chapter 3 - The First Chakra (The Root Chakra)

Description

The first Chakra is located at the bottom of the spine and faces downwards, connecting to the earth itself. It is commonly known as the Root or Base Chakra and is sometimes referred to as the Coccyx Chakra. In Sanskrit it is called the Muladhara Chakra. Red is the color associated with the Chakra and its element is Earth.

This Chakra is all about grounding and survival. Our natural urge to survive on earth is rooted deeply in all of us and is an instinctive urge that reaches back in time to a point well beyond recorded history. Survival, the need for food, shelter and security is an instinct that we share with all creatures and is a truly universal instinct. While it's a very human instinct it is also more than human. Our need for survival reminds us that we are part of a much wider world and universe.

The Root Chakra also governs our connection with the Earth, our groundedness and sense of being in the here and now. It's a very practical Chakra and generates a sense of being part of the world around us and also a sense of being 'real'. Feeling safe, stable, secure and comfortable with ourselves in the world are all connected to this Chakra. The Root Chakra is about being comfortable in your own skin and also within your immediate environment.

The needs of the physical body are very much central to this Chakra; those with a fully functioning Root Chakra pay close attention to the needs of their physical body – they exercise regularly, eat healthily and spend plenty of time out of doors in the natural world. At home they display a sense of organization and are the type of individuals that are normally in control of their paperwork and other practical aspects of life. A well attuned Root Chakra creates an important grounding for balancing the other Chakras and the simple physical focus of this Chakra creates energy, enthusiasm and the ability to cope with the challenges of life.

Imbalances within the Root Chakra

Imbalances in this Chakra have deep implications for the functioning of the other Chakras. While each must function fully and effectively, an imbalance in the Root Chakra will impact severely on the other six main Chakras. Lack of stability in the physical world is often the cause of problems with this Chakra. Stability is important to us in our early lives and problems with the Root Chakra can often be traced to events in our early lives. The loss of a parent early in life through death or divorce will contribute to feelings of insecurity and uncertainty. Those who came from backgrounds in which parents were absent for periods of time, were aggressive or violent, will normally suffer from some blockages within the Root Chakra. If your basic physical needs were not met early in life you will almost certainly need to work on balancing this Chakra to develop a strong sense of security in the here and now.

Minor imbalances in this Chakra do not always have major affects, nor do they have massive implications. You may find that you don't focus as much as you should on life's practicalities; this can manifest from simple things such as getting some, but not enough, physical exercise, to skipping meals or to simply not being great at dealing with bills, money or taxes!

If the imbalance becomes more pronounced it's likely that you'll find it difficult to deal with practical matters and will also have a sense that you are not in control of these. This can lead to a strong feeling of stress (stress is linked closely to lack of control). Anxiety and general feelings of fearfulness will often accompany stress and, in more extreme cases, a feeling of simply not being able to cope will often become apparent.

Severe imbalances in this Chakra should be dealt with as a priority. Eating disorders are linked to this Chakra; eating too much, poor quality food and weight gain can result from an overactive Root Chakra, while under-activity often manifests as Anorexia. Those with a very active Root Chakra can also be aggressive and domineering – in extremes this can manifest as physical violence. For those with a severe imbalance the priority may be to seek counseling – as the reasons for the imbalance are likely to be deeply rooted in childhood. This is a first step and as you begin to deal with issues you can also start to look at altering habits which will foster a better level of energy in your Root Chakra.

The Root Chakra Test

Use the following test to discover if your Chakra is balanced, over-active or under-active.

Use the following numbers to find your score:

1. Slightly Agree
2. Agree
3. Strongly Agree

The Questions:

- I feel unsafe in my home and the local area
- I lack self-confidence
- I become very angry, very quickly
- I have a high sex drive
- I have been homeless in the past or have moved many times
- I have a poor sense of smell
- I find it difficult to deal with basic practicalities in life
- I am often short of money

- I did not have contact (or a good relationship) with one or both parents

- I frequently become anxious for no clear reason

- I am very overweight

- I have limited appetite and struggle to enjoy food

If you have scored between 12 and 19 your Chakra is under-active. Between 20 and 30 your Chakra is in balance. From 31 to 48 your Chakra is over-active. Obviously, within each range there is some variation. If you've scored close to two ranges (either low to normal or normal to high) then you may want to consider some adjustments to your lifestyle. Retest yourself frequently to check your progress.

Balancing the Root Chakra

Your root Chakra is all about connection with the Earth, nature, with physicality and exercise. Focusing on activities that promote good balance in this Chakra is fairly straightforward.

Dance; yes, even in the kitchen with the blinds down and the doors locked! Bounce and jump to your favorite tunes and simply enjoy being present in the very energetic moment.

Walk; out of doors, in the fresh air, whatever the weather. Connect with the elements, go paddling in the sea or a river. Wander in a forest and listen to the song of the birds and the rustle of trees.

Plant a garden; or a pot of plants, herbs or vegetables. Work in a volunteer run garden if you've no outdoor space of your own.

Experience your sensuality; add salts, fragrances to your bath, have a spa treatment, or massage.

De-clutter your home and simply sit down and deal with some paperwork. Set up a filing system to deal with household bills, sell off old unused items. Clean the oven, clean the kitchen, clean the whole house. This Chakra is very much about the real practicalities of life.

Examine your diet and learn, re-learn, or simply cook a bit more. Use fresh, organic ingredients. Enjoy the process, the smells and the finished product. Get your hands and kitchen messy in the process, then clean up thoroughly afterwards.

Exercise, of the very physical kind can help to balance this Chakra particularly effectively. Take up martial arts, rugby, swimming or gymnastics.

Chapter 4 - The Second Chakra (Sacral Chakra)

Description

The Third, or Sacral, Chakra focuses on our relationship to the world and people around us. While the first, the Root Chakra, links us to the fundamental forces of the Earth, the Sacral Chakra is devoted to our relationships with the social, human world around us. The Chakra is also devoted to physical pleasure, emotional pleasure and sexuality. Our happiness and emotions are profoundly influenced by those around us and this Chakra helps us to process these influences and balance them. Sensual pleasure and joy are emotions that are associated with this Chakra and moderating both helps to balance the energy flow through the Sacral Chakra.

People with a balanced second Chakra are exuberant, joyful, full of life and the life and soul of any party going – even if that party is just daily life. They are enthusiastic, helpful, energetic and social. A well balanced Sacral Chakra helps you to feel involved with society and may well encourage you to work to help others in society. The Chakra is located close to the genital area and is often considered the 'sexual' Chakra, though this is an oversimplification. It's more accurately considered the Chakra of intimacy and involvement – of connection on a deeper level with those around us, be that in an intimate and sexual relationship, or a deeply bonded friendship. The energy of this Chakra is subtle and complex and should be considered a vital Chakra in terms of our ability to interact with those close to us and the wider world.

Imbalances within the Chakra

Signs that there are imbalance in this Chakra include an over or under active sexuality. The inability to form close, deep and loving bonds with partners is often a symptom of imbalance in this Chakra. Those who feel shy, withdrawn and who do not mix well in any social situation (work or pleasure) are likely to have a poorly performing second Chakra. Fear of change and formality with people often manifest in this case and the lack of desire to connect socially is often present.

If the second Chakra is over-performing the symptoms tend to include an inability to find joy or satisfaction in life. Often this leads to issues with substance abuse or with obsessive behaviors. Addicts to alcohol, drugs or sex are likely to have a Sacral Chakra that is too active. Those who seek new thrills, or love risk, are often found to be in this category as well.

Where the most severe balance is found individuals can be sexually and emotionally abusive. The need for control of those around them can become pronounced and can even become apparent through violence and physical abuse. These are at the most extreme end of the scale and those who feel that they fall into this category should seek professional help from a doctor or psychoanalyst.

The Sacral Chakra Test

Use the following numbers to find your score:

- Slightly Agree

- Agree

- Strongly Agree

The Questions:

- I regularly smoke, drink or take drugs

- I over-eat on a regular basis

- I take risks and enjoy high-risk sports

- I am very shy and avoid meeting new people

- I was taught to think of sex as 'dirty'

- I am constantly looking for new sexual partners

- I rarely treat myself and am embarrassed when others treat me

- I am sexually inactive and afraid of intimacy

- I feel that my life is empty and find it hard to experience joy

- I often experience violent emotions in relation to others

- I am physically violent on occasion

- I find it difficult to assert myself

If you have scored between 12 and 19 your Chakra is under-active. Between 20 and 30 your Chakra is in balance. From 31 to 48 your Chakra is over-active. Obviously, within each range there is some variation. If you've scored close to two ranges (either low to normal or normal to high) then you may want to consider some adjustments to your lifestyle. Retest yourself frequently to check your progress.

Balancing the Sacral Chakra

Balancing this Chakra will help you to overcome difficulties in many areas of life related to your interactions with other people. Here are some activities which will encourage a better balance of energy in the Sacral Chakra.

Splash out on an exotic meal. Enjoy the tastes, scents, aromas and colors of the food. Look around you and take in the visual experiences too.

Chat with a friend. Talk about your problems, your achievements. Listen to their conversation. Laugh together.

Activities associated with water are very beneficial to the Sacral Chakra; from taking a scented bath to sea kayaking (and most things in between). Enjoy the challenge and the sensation of being in, around or near water. Simply find a stream and listen to the way it splutters and chatters over the stones.

Learn to dance; go to classes, be willing to laugh at yourself or surprise yourself. Combining this kind of physical activity with a social one can help to develop a sense of intimacy and trust with a wider group of people.

Learn about your inner child. Joy, sheer and unadulterated joy, is what this Chakra is about; go to a funfair and scare yourself silly with laughter on the rides.

Paint, draw, knit or crochet and give your creations away to friends, neighbors and family.

Donate some time to a local charity or group to help out those less fortunate than yourself.

Chapter 5 - The Third Chakra (Solar Plexus Chakra)

Description

The Solar Plexus is closely linked to will power and assertiveness. It has links to our sense of control in life – or complete lack of it! The solar plexus is about making yourself the driving force in your life, about choosing where you wish to be in life and the route you choose to get there. The element that is associated with this Chakra is fire; fire can be a great force for change, for security and for good. It can also be destructive if not handled carefully. A well balanced Solar Plexus Chakra will help you to achieve your goals in life – although not at the expense of others. It will give you the energy and focus to achieve your dreams and to be firm about your goals and maintaining your progress towards them, without being dissuaded by those around your or disheartened by thoughts of failure. Your actions will be underpinned by determination and will contribute to the success of your endeavors. A balanced third Chakra helps you to steer life in the direction you want but also gives you a flexible personality which helps to adjust your plans if life throws obstacles in your way.

Challenges are one thing that you will find that you enjoy when your third Chakra is in balance and you'll thrive on these to a great extent. Challenges in life can help us to learn and grow and, ultimately, foster a greater sense of self-control and self-determination. Self-respect and a well balanced third Chakra also go hand in hand; you won't easily be taken advantage of but at the same time will be compassionate with others and keen to help them in their own lives, struggles and in dealing with lack of confidence. Those with a well balanced Solar Plexus are likely to be successful in life – rarely will they be overnight success but their achievements will be built on firm foundations, the sort that create lasting successes. There is a strong connection with instinct and the Solar Plexus Chakra; gut feelings, instinctual actions and an intuitive knowledge of how to deal with both challenges and opportunities come with a correctly attuned Solar Plexus Chakra.

Imbalances within the Solar Plexus Chakra

Imbalances in this Chakra manifest in a number of ways; a low level of activity in this Chakra will appear as low self-confidence, a fearful personality, one unwilling to take risks or uncomfortable with making decisions. Those with a highly active Solar Plexus Chakra will usually be bullying, domineering and determined to achieve their goals whatever the implications for others around them. Workaholics often fall into this category and while capable of high achieving, often sacrifice friends and family in the process. Some people will display both extremes, an imbalanced Solar Plexus can swing between both, creating a complex personality who, in the end, often fails to achieve any of their goals.

Those with imbalances in this Chakra will often fear authority – expressing that fear in either of the fight or flight responses. They often express desires to have a different career from that which they are currently in, but seem unable to make the change. Sometimes they will cite outside influences as diverting them from their 'real' path in life, unwilling to take control themselves and direct their own destinies. Lacking in self-confidence will also often mean that you are afraid of what others may think of you and be overly conventional in your approach to life. Problem solving or dealing with challenges can also be difficult for those who have a poorly performing third Chakra.

Aggressive, manipulative and explosive characters often have severe imbalances in their Solar Plexus Chakra. Hungry for power or success they will be manipulative, possibly outright threatening. Those with Obsessive Compulsive Disorder may also have a severely overactive third Chakra.

Imbalances in this Chakra can be caused by a huge range of influences in life. Poor, inadequate schooling, abusive or absent parents and lack of guidance in early life often result in both extremes associated with an under-performing Solar Plexus. For those who have not had early opportunities in life, have become trapped in unsatisfactory careers or relationships, improving the activity and balance of this Chakra can have a profound and very positive effect.

The Solar Plexus Test

Use the following test to discover if your Chakra is balanced, over-active or under-active.

Use the following numbers to find your score:

- Slightly Agree

- Agree

- Strongly Agree

The Questions:

- I often give into the requests or demand that others place on me.

- I am very unhappy with my job but don't know how to change the situation

- I don't like fighting for what I want and avoid confrontation in life

- I have never passed my driving test

- I was physically abused during childhood

- I have been physically violent in an adult relationship

- I feel I am unable to change my circumstances

- I bite my nails and have other nervous traits

- I always feel the need to be in control

- I prefer others to make major decisions in life

- I don't feel that I have the life I planned but don't know how to take steps to change this

- I find it difficult to deal with those in authority (avoiding this or becoming confrontational)

If you have scored between 12 and 19 your Chakra is under-active. Between 20 and 30 your Chakra is in balance. From 31 to 48 your Chakra is over-active. Obviously, within each range there is some variation. If you've scored close to two ranges (either low to normal or normal to high) then you may want to consider some adjustments to your lifestyle. Retest yourself frequently to check your progress.

Activities to Improve

If you can't already, learn to drive. If you can, but don't often, take a long drive to a new region you've not visited before.

Redecorate a room. Choose the colors, the style and furnishings. Do the work yourself and sit back and enjoy the fruits of your planning, executing and accomplishment.

Learn a new skill. This can be anything you have always wanted to master, a language, a creative or practical skill.

Have a bonfire; burn old, unwanted items that you feel have negative associations.

Mia Rose & Priya Sareeh

Think about your goals in life; identify each one and also how you can create steps towards achieving each one. Take one goal at a time, never try to do everything at once as that is a perfect recipe to fail!

Chapter 6 - The Fourth Chakra (The Heart Chakra)

Description

The Heart Chakra or the fourth Chakra is the central Chakra; it creates a link between the three lower and three upper Chakras. The focus of these Chakras is different – the lower Chakras relating to the physical world, the body and our own personality. The three upper Chakras relate more to the world of intellect, expression and spirituality. The Heart Chakra creates a link between these different Chakras; forming a place where the physical and the cerebral or spiritual persona links.

Our physical heart keeps us alive, pumping blood around our body to provide nutrients. Our Heart Chakra is crucial in translating physical and spiritual experiences in our lives and in balancing in these. Our physical health and mental or emotional health are strongly linked (modern medicine and psychoanalysts will not disagree with this). The Heart Chakra process the very human experiences of pain, love, suffering and compassion. It balances these emotions and experiences keeping them from affecting us physically or mentally in excess.

This Chakra is keenly associated with love; not just romantic love but parental and also a wider, social sense of the word, best understood as compassion, or humanity. Love is, or should be, unconditional, seeking neither reward nor reciprocation. In this sense, love means respect and care of the world and the people around us.

Those with a well balanced Heart Chakra appear as honest, open and interested individuals. They don't hide things about themselves and share their experiences openly. They have a well developed self-acceptance and this translates into a genuine lack of judgment when it comes to others; this type of individual is accepting of those from different backgrounds, races, religions or those with different lifestyles. Accepting yourself, loving yourself, is the first step on the road to a much wider acceptance of others and, also, to gaining the trust and acceptance of others.

Imbalances within the Heart Chakra

The Heart Chakra is linked to the element air. Those with imbalances may find that they have recurring lung or breathing problems. Asthma and similar conditions are believed to be manifestations of an imbalance in the Heart Chakra. For those with an overactive fourth Chakra, putting others before oneself is a common trait. While this can be an admirable trait it can also be damaging. Constantly denying your own needs and putting others before you is draining and can lead to listlessness, resentment and isolation. It can leave you open to manipulation by others. Those with an under-active Heart Chakra often display coldness in their dealings with others and a lack of empathy. Closing yourself off to others, focusing only on your needs and feeling vulnerable when love is shown by others is also a sign that your Heart Chakra needs to be balanced more effectively.

Those with a poorly performing Heart Chakra find it difficult to build close personal relationships and often experience strong feelings of loneliness even when surrounded by many people. An unbalanced fourth Chakra is a sign of those who lack self-love. This is not a selfish emotion but one which accepts the self, loving yourself for who you are, despite any and every fault. Apart from emotional issues the imbalances in this Chakra can lead to heart disease, angina, stroke and circulatory problems. It's interesting to note that modern medicine has recently accepted that there are links between heart disease, and some cancers, that loneliness can exacerbate.

Lack of love in early life, rejection or loss of a loved one as a child can all contribute to a blocked fourth Chakra. Low self-esteem, belief that you are physically unattractive, dissatisfaction with looks or your own personality can all also lead to problems with the Heart Chakra. Often rejection (divorce or separation) will create a whole range of problems with self-esteem and self-worth. Over time these can become more serious and it is crucial that you should seek some form of counseling in order to allow your Heart Chakra to heal.

The Heart Chakra Test

Use the following test to discover if your Chakra is balanced, over-active or under-active.

Use the following numbers to find your score:

- Slightly Agree
- Agree
- Strongly Agree

The Questions:

- I become bitter if I feel I have been slighted
- I do not forgive easily
- I do not willing give gifts, time or money to others
- I frequently become jealous of others
- I do not feel that I love my partner anymore but am afraid of being alone
- I think that my partner is unfaithful and am constantly afraid of this
- I have difficulty in being honest with people about how I am feeling
- I am not interested in social problems or willing to do voluntary work
- I tend to put other peoples' needs before my own

- I find I have little time for myself

- I believe I am ugly/too fat or just unattractive

- I lost a close relative before I was seven years old

If you have scored between 12 and 19 your Chakra is under-active. Between 20 and 30 your Chakra is in balance. From 31 to 48 your Chakra is over-active. Obviously, within each range there is some variation. If you've scored close to two ranges (either low to normal or normal to high) then you may want to consider some adjustments to your lifestyle. Retest yourself frequently to check your progress.

Balancing the Heart Chakra

Learn to forgive yourself and others. We all make mistakes, we often make many throughout our lives. It's human, and you are allowed to move on!

Take some time each week to treat yourself, just yourself. Go shopping, take a spa treatment or simply sit down with a book in a quiet place and don't allow interruptions.

Find a local volunteer group; working with the homeless is a good activity for the Heart Chakra, it broadens your understanding of the issues and encourages you to reach out to people from backgrounds you may not normally encounter. Visit a pet sanctuary and consider offering a new, loving, stable home to an abandoned animal.

Take up exercise if you don't regularly do so already; up your game if you do. Physical exercise is good for the physical heart and also the Heart Chakra.

Look at the positive things that you have in your life and accept that you cannot have everything in life.

Look in the mirror, look yourself in the eye and tell yourself that you are beautiful.

Tell someone you love them, forgive a friend for a mistake.

Throw a dinner party and buy the best, most expensive ingredients to share with your friends and family.

Chapter 7 - The Fifth Chakra (The Throat Chakra)

Description

This Chakra, the fifth, lying above the Heart Chakra and associated with the throat is the first of the three higher Chakras. These Chakras relate to communication, intellect and spirituality. The Throat Chakra is related to communication, including writing, speaking and the ability to express oneself. In this latter sense 'communication' is at its broadest and this Chakra relates strongly to self-expression and being who you truly are.

Those with a strong, well balanced Chakra are identified by their abilities to understand and express their own needs. They express themselves clearly in a calm, non-threatening way and are often excellent teachers, writers and musicians. The Throat Chakra is not only about verbal communication but very much about the ability to communicate your inner emotions, thoughts and feelings in a variety of ways.

One important trait of those with a well-balanced Throat Chakra is their ability to listen. Indeed, good communicators instinctively understand that communication is a two-way process and that in order to effectively communicate you must be able to listen and truly hear what others are trying to say. Expressive, creative, excellent at listening and analyzing, those with good balance in this Chakra also make excellent counselors and analysts. Whether in a professional sense, or not, it is those with a balanced Throat Chakra that we seek when we need a friend to listen to our problems. It is also this type of person who offers the best advice – advice that we willingly listen to.

Imbalances within the Throat Chakra

Imbalances in the Throat Chakra are easily identified in others; those who are very talkative and often seem dogmatic or arrogant have a Fifth Chakra which is over-performing. Gossiping, poor listening skills and frequently interrupting others in conversation are also signs that your Throat Chakra is over-performing. Many with a imbalanced Throat Chakra will come across as boring in conversation, they are unable to express themselves simply and in a concise way, resulting in a rambling, unclear approach to any conversation!

Often viewed as shy, retiring and timid those with an under-performing Fifth Chakra find it hard to make themselves heard. They prefer not to speak and while they may be very good listeners may not participate beyond listening in conversation. They tend to undervalue their own opinion, often seeing right to the heart of a matter but being unwilling to express their (valuable) opinions. In this category people tend to prefer others to do the talking for them – choosing professions where public speaking is avoidable and partners who are garrulous and enjoy doing most of the communicating in a relationship.

The most severe imbalances in the Fifth Chakra express themselves in terms of anger and rage. Opinions become extreme and those who find it hard to communicate a point, without controlling the conversation, may have a severe imbalance in this Chakra. Anger management classes can be of great benefit in this case – and classes focused on communication can also be very beneficial.

Use the following test to discover if your Chakra is balanced, over-active or under-active. Score yourself as follows;

The Throat Chakra Test

Use the following test to discover if your Chakra is balanced, over-active or under-active.

Use the following numbers to find your score:

- Slightly Agree

- Agree

- Strongly Agree

The Questions:

- I have had a throat injury.

- I do not like involving myself in debate or engaging in arguments

- I keep my opinions to myself to avoid hurting or upsetting others

- People have told me I am over-critical or judgmental

- I have a low voice which people struggle to hear

- I often have to explain what I want more than once

- I avoid speaking in groups or avoid public speaking

- I often lose my temper violently in conversation/discussion

- I am very talkative and don't spend much time listening

- I tell lies to protect myself, or others, frequently

- I will agree with people rather than discuss or argue

- I am often a source of advice but feel I am unable to express my own needs

If you have scored between 12 and 19 your Chakra is under-active. Between 20 and 30 your Chakra is in balance. From 31 to 48 your Chakra is over-active. Obviously, within each range there is some variation. If you've scored close to two ranges (either low to normal or normal to high) then you may want to consider some adjustments to your lifestyle. Retest yourself frequently to check your progress.

Balancing the Throat Chakra

Sing; even if you can't! If you can, join a choir but if you are not confident, then sing at the top of your voice in the car to the radio or your own music.

Talk to yourself. If you find it difficult to communicate with others practice by talking as if you were trying to get a message across to someone. Practice makes perfect in communication.

Massage – particularly focusing on the upper back and neck is great for the shoulders and throat, relaxing muscles and tendons. For the throat Chakra this can be a simple, practical technique to foster improvement.

Sit in silence and listen to the world around you. Try this in a quiet, peaceful location and a busy, noisy location. Listen closely to all the sounds you encounter.

Write down your feelings and emotions. Learn to translate what is going on inside into a real, solid form in the world. This is a crucial skill for developing communication skills and a balanced Throat Chakra.

Flotation tanks can be a great way to work on the Throat and other upper Chakras. They remove the immediate, physical experience of daily life and allow us to focus on the higher, intellectual parts of ourselves.

Make time for conversation, with friends or family, without interruptions. Go for a meal, have a chat and talk to a stranger on the bus or in the park (choose your stranger carefully!)

Chapter 8 - The Sixth Chakra (The Third Eye)

Description

Following on from our self-expressive nature embodied in the Fifth Chakra we move more into our intellectual and intuitive abilities. The Sixth, penultimate Chakra, is also known as the Third Eye. This is one of the most complex Chakras to understand, in many senses. While it relates to our intellectual powers it also is strongly linked to our spiritual and intuitive selves. The focus of this Chakra is on decision making but not in the traditionally understood sense, but rather in the sense of using our whole selves to make decisions that are right for us.

Functioning correctly this Chakra works on some level with each of the Chakras and enables us to tune into our higher selves. Those with a correctly functioning Third Eye are intuitive individuals who find that they instinctively 'know' things without being told. They can clearly visualize their lives and the path that life is taking them on as well as being able to make decisions based as much on intuition as on a practical level.

Decision making is important in life but making decisions that allow you to remain true to yourself and those that are also ethical and right for you is crucial. This is the role in which the Third Eye plays an important part. Those with an open, well balanced third eye often feel that they experience clairvoyance (which literally translates as clear-seeing and is a very apt description), deja-vu and precognition. Many also experience auditory and visual phenomena that are predictive in nature.

Related to decision making and intellect, the Third Eye is wider in scope and being open to gut instinct or intuitive, emotion based decision making is a strong feature in those who have a well-balanced sixth Chakra. This broader approach to intellect provides an open mind and attitude to life which is at the same time both accepting and inquiring. In balance the Third Chakra is a valuable asset for leading a life in which dealing with problems and challenges can become simple, straightforward and less stressful.

Imbalances within the Third Eye Chakra

Imbalances in this Chakra can have a profound affect on our lives. Often people who over-rationalize decisions, or feel that fact based reasoning is the only way in which to solve problems, have a blocked energy field in this Chakra. Reasoning using logic and facts are very sound methods but those who cannot bring an intuitive level to evaluating decision often make poor decisions. Some decisions may be correct factually but just feel wrong.

Those with obsessive compulsive disorder and other obsessive behaviors frequently have an imbalance in this Chakra. Over active Third Eyes often lead to excessive visualization, imagination and even delusions. Those who suffer headaches and migraine may also have a Third Eye which is out of balance. The Chakra is also linked to many forms of mental illness – either through under-performing or over-performing. OCD, or rigidity in thinking, will result from a poorly performing Third Eye while serious mental illness, such as schizophrenia, may develop in those with an over-performing Chakra. These issues should be addressed by professionals in a medical or psychoanalytic setting, while Chakra therapy should be considered as a good grounding and secondary therapy.

The Third Eye Test

Use the following test to discover if your Chakra is balanced, over-active or under-active.

Use the following numbers to find your score:

- Slightly Agree

- Agree

- Strongly Agree

The Questions:
- I have difficulty concentrating for long periods

- I rarely make plans for the future

- I am not interested in or involved in spirituality in any way
- I rarely dream or remember my dreams
- I often obsess over details in life
- I believe that psychics and mystics are superstitious
- I believe in science over all things
- Decisions should be made purely on facts
- I daydream frequently
- I fear death and often worry about this
- I frequently hear voices when nobody is there
- I have made many poor decisions in my past

If you have scored between 12 and 19 your Chakra is under-active. Between 20 and 30 your Chakra is in balance. From 31 to 48 your Chakra is over-active. Obviously, within each range there is some variation. If you've scored close to two ranges (either low to normal or normal to high) then you may want to consider some adjustments to your lifestyle. Retest yourself frequently to check your progress.

Balancing the Third Eye Chakra

Keep a diary of your dreams and mediate on these to evaluate what your higher self is trying to tell you.

Ensure that you are getting enough, healthy sleep. If necessary talk to a doctor or therapist about this and develop good sleep practices.

Meditation and Yoga are strongly advised to help develop a strong Third Eye. Both are now widely recognized by the medical profession as beneficial for health in general, so even if you are skeptical give them a try!

Spend a little time each evening to evaluate and reflect on your day. Think through any decisions you've made and see how you feel about these emotionally.

Be spontaneous. Get in the car, on a bus, or take a walk. Allow your intuition to guide you and try not to consciously make decisions about where you are going.

Buy some new clothes and, again, let your intuition rule your choices.

Our brains are far more powerful than we realize; practice guessing or sensing who is calling when the phone rings. You'll be surprised at the results as you become more experienced.

Spend time with animals, most communicate in non-verbal ways. Learn to 'read' what they are trying to tell you.

Chapter 9 The Seventh Chakra (The Crown Chakra)

Description

The Crown, or Seventh Chakra, is the last of the main Chakras and concentrates on the last significant part of our lives. This Chakra is identified with our spiritual selves and our ability to achieve higher states of consciousness and perception. For many, in an age in which religion and spirituality has lost its place, this can be the hardest Chakra to access and balance. Some people argue that in the modern world there is little place for spirituality. However, throughout history, from our very earliest days, religious expression of some kind has played a key role in not only our daily lives but our development as humans. To discount it may not be wise and to recognize it on some level, if only in our intimate connection to the rest of the world around us may be important for society as a whole and for our ability to function in life as individuals.

In the Chakra tradition the Crown and the soul are perceived as inextricably linked. The belief is held that it is through the Crown that our soul enters the body at the start of our lives and through the crown that it departs at the end. Through the Crown we connect not only with all other people around us but also with the wider universe. There can be no argument from most scientific quarters that we are all expressions of simple energy at an atomic level. This energy continues to exist beyond our own lifespans and has existed long before we came into being. In the Chakra tradition this has long been acknowledged in terms of the Crown Chakra and it is in this Chakra we are linked to that wider existence.

Those with a fully balanced Crown Chakra are open, giving and selfless. They do not view themselves in isolation to the world but simply as one expression of creation and existence. They will frequently be found amongst activists working to protect the environment, working to eliminate poverty or to better the lives of others in some way. Those striving to affect change in the world, change for the better, are amongst those who have a balanced, open Crown Chakra. In this sense the Crown Chakra need not be equated with spirituality or religion but simply with an altruistic nature which strives to create a greater level of equality and sustainability in the world. As you balance your Crown Chakra it is, however, likely that your perception of the spiritual will develop in a positive way.

Imbalances within the Crown Chakra

Those with an imbalance in the Crown Chakra may experience high levels of cynicism about belief systems. Under-performing Crown Chakras often find expression in either non-belief or very rigid belief systems. Those who are not open to different aspects of belief and spirituality expressed by religions or traditions that are unfamiliar to them often have a blocked, under-performing Crown Chakra.

Over-performing Crown Chakras often denote those who are excessively materialistic, greedy and put themselves before others in all situations. Physical pleasures come high on their list of meaningful experiences but they often find that these pleasures don't ultimately deliver any real satisfaction. Worldly, cynical and often disillusioned with life, re-balancing the Crown Chakra can help many to see beyond themselves and find a deeper satisfaction in life.

The Crown Chakra Test

Use the following test to discover if your Chakra is balanced, over-active or under-active.

Use the following numbers to find your score:

- Slightly Agree

- Agree

- Strongly Agree

The Questions:

- I often feel lonely, whether physically alone or amongst others

- I do not believe in God, spirituality or the divine

- I have little interest in the environment or environmental issues

- I believe you only live once and enjoying this life is paramount

- Prayer is of no use and cannot achieve any practical ends

- I was not brought up in a religious family

- I feel that my own life is meaningless

- I focus on acquiring material possessions

- I often feel disillusioned with life and disinterested in those around me

- I am not interested in the fate of others in different parts of the world

- Life can only be understood through science and intellectual points of view

If you have scored between 12 and 19 your Chakra is under-active. Between 20 and 30 your Chakra is in balance. From 31 to 48 your Chakra is over-active. Obviously, within each range there is some variation. If you've scored close to two ranges (either low to normal or normal to high) then you may want to consider some adjustments to your lifestyle. Retest yourself frequently to check your progress.

Balancing the Crown Chakra

Balancing your other Chakras is actually a crucial aspect of achieving balance in the Crown Chakra. In many cases as the other Chakras come into balance the Crown begins to develop its own balance.

If you have no grounding in religion consider studying a course in a faith or religious tradition. For those who find traditional religious structures difficult, learn a little about Buddhism or the Hindu religions.

Find time for silence in your life; religious buildings are good for this, when not in use. Remote countryside and empty beaches are also great places to simply sit and let your thoughts quieten down.

Learn a language – particularly one that is very foreign! This can help to change the way in which you think, creating new patterns and links in your brain.

Meditation and Yoga are both very good tools to develop healthy balance in all of the Chakras and will encourage improvements in the Crown Chakra.

> Read in full; The Bible, The Koran, The Torah, The Vedas and key Buddhist texts. If you are critical of religious traditions you may as well know the facts! You may be surprised at some of the similarities too.

Chapter 10 - Additional Chakra Information

In this final chapter we take a look at several aspects that can help to balance the Chakras. Traditionally certain colors, sounds, crystals, essential oils have been associated with each Chakra. Not everyone will feel that using these techniques is useful but, as you develop a fuller understanding and appreciation of the Chakras, you may find that these 'tools' will help to balance your Chakras and also maintain that balance. The sound listed is commonly used to form a Mantra, a repetitive chanting of the sound which aids in meditation, relaxation and can be beneficial to the associated Chakra. This chapter provides a list for each Chakra and can be used as a basis for your own research.

The First Chakra – The Root Chakra

- Color Association: Red
- Note: C
- Sound: Lam
- Crystals: Garnet, Ruby, Jasper and Smokey Quartz
- Oils: Patchouli, myrrh and cypress

- Solfeggio Frequency 396Hz

The Second Chakra – The Sacral Chakra

- Color Association: Orange
- Note: D
- Sound: Vam
- Crystals: Coral, Citrine, Amber and Carnelian
- Oils: Orange, rosemary and juniper
- Solfeggio Frequency 417Hz

The Third Chakra – The Solar Plexus Chakra

- Color Association: Yellow
- Note: E
- Sound: Ram
- Crystals: Gold Calcite, Tiger's Eye and Yellow Topaz
- Oils Ylang-Ylang, Bergamot and Lavender
- Solfeggio Frequency 528Hz

The Fourth Chakra – The Heart Chakra

- Color Association: Green
- Note: F
- Sound: Yam
- Crystals: Rose Quartz, Emerald and Malachite
- Oils   Rose, Sage and Sandal Wood
- Solfeggio Frequency   639Hz

The Fifth Chakra – The Throat Chakra

- Color Association: Blue
- Note: G
- Sound: Ham
- Crystals: Blue Topaz, Lapis Lazuli and Sapphire
- Oils   Lavender and Patchouli
- Solfeggio Frequency   741Hz

The Sixth Chakra – The Throat Chakra

- Color Association: Indigo

- Note: A
- Sound: Aum (Om)
- Crystals: Quartz, Amethyst and Azurite
- Oils: Juniper, Peppermint and geranium
- Solfeggio Frequency 852Hz

The Seventh Chakra – The Crown Chakra

- Color Association: Violet
- Note: B
- Sound: None (Aum is sometimes used)
- Crystals: Amethyst, Diamonds and Clear Quartz
- Oils: Jasmine, Frankincense and Lotus
- Solfeggio Frequency 963Hz*

*This frequency does not appear in traditional musical scales but is an additional scale at a higher frequency.

The crystals, oils, sounds and colors associated with each Chakra can be used during meditation or simply utilized in daily life when working to balance or maintain an individual Chakra. With crystal the color association is important and other crystals not listed can also be employed in improving the flow of energy within the relevant Chakra.

Conclusion

Thank you again for reading this book!

I hope this book has given you insight into your own sign of the Zodiac and that of your friends and family and also highlighted some areas which are overlooked in modern Astrology.

Finally, if you enjoyed this book, please take the time to share your thoughts and post a review on Amazon. It'd be greatly appreciated!

Thank you and good luck!

Mia Rose & Priya Sareeh

Mudras for weight loss

25 Simple Hand Gestures for Weight Loss - A Beginners Guide To Mudras

Written By
Priya Sareeh

Introduction

I want to thank you and congratulate you for getting the book, "Mudras for Weight Loss".

This book contains proven steps and strategies on how to use the ancient art of Mudras to achieve long term weight loss and a healthier life.

Mudras are closely linked to Yoga and are found in widespread use in cultures influenced by Vedic and Buddhist traditions. They can be found in the practice of meditation, in dance and are also applied in medical settings. The power of the mind and the body, when working together is far more powerful than any super-pill or dieting method and in this book we look at just how you can use this ancient practice to lose weight and keep that weight off, for good! The book contains information on the background behind Mudras but the main focus and larger part of the book, is devoted to descriptions of the Mudras you will need to aid healthy and successful weight loss.

Thanks again for reading this book, I hope you enjoy it!

Mia Rose & Priya Sareeh

Chapter 1 - Weight Loss; a Big Problem

Weight loss; it's a hot topic and one that many people battle with for years. From celebrity diets to pills and potions there are no end of options when it comes to losing the pounds and achieving a healthy weight. So, with all these options, why do so many people battle with weight? While starting the latest fad diet is easy enough, staying with it, maintaining it and avoiding all the temptations of easily and readily available food in the modern world, seems much harder. Many of us find ourselves stuck in a cycle of weight loss, weight gain and weight loss.

There are several reasons for this and, often, the reasons vary widely in individual cases. Food, in Western cultures, is not only more readily available than ever before, it's also processed beyond all recognition in many instances. In order to preserve, add a bit of color and keep us wanting more, our food is also subject to a startling array of additives and chemicals which make it less a processed product and more of an embalmed one. Many of the additives in modern food are not only unnatural but most have some serious health implications and many include additives and ingredients which create addictions. It would be cynical to say that this is to ensure we keep on coming back for more, but it might be true.

Whatever the truth, high-fat, high-sugar and low-energy value foods have become the norm for most of us. While we may try to battle the cravings and the hunger that these foods create, our own bodies fight against using a range of chemicals (hormones) to make us angry, to create cravings and to mistakenly think we are starving. While some people manage to lose weight effortlessly, many of us try (and fail) repeatedly before find some success. Yet more of us never really find that success and remain trapped in a cycle of dieting, weight loss and weight gain.

There is no simple answer to beating this cycle and dieting, or dieting alone, can be as much part of the problem as it is the solution. In recent years both medical professionals and nutritionists have conducted extensive research into how we can break the cycle. This is for many reasons but the two important ones are simply that obesity kills and the cost of health-care for those affected by the condition is spiraling out of control. On its own, obesity may not kill you but the related conditions which it creates most probably will.

One interesting fact to note about 21st century health-care, from many perspectives and for many conditions, is that it takes a more balanced approach to treatment. Sometimes called "holistic" this new approach looks at lifestyle issues, social issues, psychological issues and the broader context in which we live. In general, the latest approach to treating a large number of conditions aims to achieve all round balance in all areas of our life, rather than simply dealing with one issue as if it were unrelated to the rest of our personality or life.

This isn't, of course, a new approach. For many hundreds (and even thousands of years) several cultures have taken this approach. In the East, in particular, certain belief systems have focused their religious and medical practices on treating each person as a whole, rather than a sum of parts. Many of these belief systems have also heavily influenced other areas of life, including our health. Ancient Chinese, Indian and Japanese cultures all have aspects of this understanding and the health of the body, the soul and the mind have not been seen as separate parts of a whole but interrelated components of that whole.

Today, many people are looking into these traditions with deeper understanding and their teachings and methods are not being dismissed in quiet the way they were. From using mindfulness, an ancient form of meditation to treat depression; right through to using Mudras to assist with weight loss. The brave new world of modern medicine is beginning to recognize that listening to your elders doesn't always mean having to take on board a lot of garbled nonsense!

The subject of this book is losing weight through the use of Mudras but before we get started it may be useful to take a look at what Mudras actually are, where they came from and just why they may be able to help us with achieving a healthy weight.

What are Mudras?

The word Mudra is a Sanskrit word meaning "seal", "mark" or "gesture". Sanskrit is ancient language that was once used widely in and around the Indian sub-continent; gradually it has been replaced by modern languages but remains in use in religious settings and in older philosophical and literary texts. Much like Latin, in the West, it has largely died out as a commonly used language but remains a source of authority and learning.

Today, the concept and meaning of the Mudra is found not only in India but in most cultures that have Buddhist traditions in their history. The word varies and can be found as "yin" in China or "in" in Japan and Korea. The Mudra is a "ritual gesture" marking intent, meaning and creating a promise. Similar concepts can be found in most religious contexts including other major religions (folding the hands in prayer or making the sign of the cross, for example). The gesture in all of these traditions makes a pact, a promise and signifies intent.

When Words Aren't Enough

So, if a Mudra is simply a gesture, can it have an effect on our bodies or our minds? Well, it's certainly a well-known fact that thought precedes action, that ideas are the parent of invention and actions speak louder than words! However Mudras have long been linked with the practice of Yoga – itself closely linked to Buddhist practices. Yoga is a form of meditation but also includes a strong physical element; Mudras are used within the tradition as a focus in both meditation and more physical aspects of the practice. This is where the "secret", the "magic" or the plain practical aspects of using Mudras for weight loss may lie.

In Yoga the use of Mudras is strongly linked to breathing exercises which are designed to affect the flow of "Prana" in the body. Prana is the "life force" that is referred to in many Eastern religions and also in medical traditions, representing the cosmic energy of the universe originating in the sun. Each Mudra is designed to regulate the flow of prana in our bodies to attune it with the greater universe around us. In a real sense this is about attuning our bodies and our minds with our environment. Which takes us back to where we began – learning to live in a way which balance our bodies, our minds and our spirits in a holistic way.

Can Hand Gestures Really Help Me Lose Weight?

Losing weight requires a certain amount of will power, a healthy diet and avoiding eating to excess. All of these can be achieved without Mudras; yet, with them, it can be far easier to win the weight loss battle. There are two elements to the technique; used correctly, in a meditative state, Mudras will enhance your sense of purpose and your willpower. As a sign of intent they'll help you to focus on that intent. However, there may be more to it than that (and these techniques have been practiced successfully for thousands of years – so there probably is!). Science has helped to enlighten us in many ways in recent years but there are many areas which remain unclear. The relationship between our mental state, our physical health and our abilities to gain and lose weight is as yet, not fully understood. In addition, the way in which Mudras create small, but very real, physical changes in our body, can help through meditation to modify our metabolism. Mudras may be, in effect, a micro-workout for the body but the way in which they physically affect us is still very much "gray-areas" in science. Although science has begun to accept that even small amounts of exercise can have an impact for hours after they have been practiced and can continue to burn calories at a surprising rate.

Some practices which share roots with the use of Mudras have now made their way into mainstream medical and psychological practice. In many senses, belief systems that have been dismissed by modern science for many years could be forgiven for saying "we told you so". Although, in practice, most of them have the inner peace not to do so! Mudras, for whatever reason, can and do change our bodies. They can be used alone, or with other methods, to lose weight, improve your health and restore a balance to your life that is missing.

Mia Rose & Priya Sareeh

I hope that you enjoy this book and that it can help you to achieve all of those things.

Chapter 2 - Mudras to Burn Off Excess Fat

In order to lose weight there's one important factor; you'll need to shed excess fat. In this chapter we'll look at the Mudras that should help you to achieve exactly that.

Mudra 1: Linga Mudra

Meaning and Health Benefits

This Mudra encapsulates male power, the Sanskrit word "Linga" roughly translates as "phallus". The Mudra increases body heat and is recognized as having a number of health benefits besides weight loss; these include combating colds, flu and fevers. It's believed to boost the immune system and also the respiratory system. These effects all contribute to its value as an all-round boost for your system, which in turn has a positive effect on weight loss.

Effectiveness

This Mudra is extremely effective and works quickly; it should only be practiced for a short period of time, so use it for around five to seven minutes at a time. To perform the Mudra for longer periods take a break of at least five minutes between each session. The Mudra will increase your will-power, determination and also make you more active and these reasons combined make it one of the essential Mudras for burning off excess fat.

Performing the Mudra

You can perform this Mudra in either a seated or standing position but ensure that you are comfortable before beginning. Clasp your fingers together so that they intertwine, keeping the thumb of your left hand erect and straight. Bring your hand to rest close to your abdomen and breathe in and out deeply and slowly.

Mudra 2: Rudra Mudra

Meaning and Health Benefits

This Mudra is linked to the Hindu god Shiva and is believed to help regulate the activity of the Solar Plexus Chakra. This Chakra is related to our physical desires in the world and the Mudra helps to regulate these. As such it helps to regulate the whole body and the energy that flows through it (the Prana). In this sense, the Mudra is designed to help the body achieve balance in a physical way and it's believed to help remove toxins and excess fat and also to restore a balance of energy within the body. Other than assisting with effective weight loss it also regulates blood pressure, reduces dizziness (which can be a symptom of cravings) and is also good at helping to maintain mental balance.

Effectiveness

As with the Lingra Mudra, this is a highly effective weight loss Mudra, it will work very quickly and can be performed up to six times a day. You can safely practice this Mudra for up to

40 minutes at a time but be sure to take reasonable breaks between sessions.

Performing the Mudra

For this Mudra you should be seated comfortably, ideally on the floor but a chair will be fine to start with. Either way, sit up very straight with your head held high and your chest out; use both hands to practice this Mudra. Breathe in and let your mind and body relax. Raise your hands and press the tips of each index finger, thumb and ring finger together, leaving the middle and little fingers pointing straight outwards.

Mudra 3: Surya Mudra

Meaning and Health Benefits

The Sudra Mudra is identified with the sun – the source of the cosmic energy that pervades all of creation – including ourselves. The sun is also the symbol of fire and, as such, we can understand this Mudra in terms of literally burning off excess fat with energy! The Mudra will encourage your body's metabolism to burn off excess energy, helping you to reduce your weight.

Effectiveness

As with all the Mudras that help to reduce excess fat, this is an effective and fast acting gesture. You can practice this Mudra for anything from 1five minutes to 4five minutes at a time. You can either practice one session each day (for a maximum of 4five minutes) or split the time into three 1five minute sessions. This Mudra will also raise body heat and increase the effectiveness of your metabolism. Aside from weight loss, it is believed to aid in speedy recovery from the common cold and is also used to improve physical posture.

Performing the Mudra

This Mudra can be performed in either a seated or standing position, whichever is most comfortable and, again, use both hands. Hold your hands outwards and bend the ring finger into your palm, pressing your thumb over it, your remaining fingers should be kept straight.

Chapter 3 - Developing the Digestive System

In the previous chapter we covered the most effective Mudras for getting rid of excess weight quickly. However, excess body fat is only part of the problem when it comes to dealing with weight loss. Even being overweight for a short period of time can cause chaos with our metabolism and with our digestive systems. Additionally, if you are combining the use of Mudras with a particular diet there is a strong chance that your digestive system is in a state of confusion. In this chapter we take a look at the Mudras that will help to restore balance to your digestive tract and restore normal and natural function to your body.

Mudra 4: Apaan Mudra

Meaning and Health Benefits

This Mudra symbolizes "downward force" - and for this reason it is **not recommended** for use during pregnancy, although it is used traditionally during childbirth, or when birth is delayed. In health terms, the Mudra is used for dealing with constipation, flatulence and indigestion. It purifies the body of toxins by encouraging normal digestion and bowel movements.

Effectiveness

In terms of clearing the body the Mudra is highly effective and although powerful can be used regularly and long term to continue to reap the benefits it bestows. The Mudra should be practiced for 30 minutes, although you can split this time into 1five minute sessions if you prefer. Ideally, perform these sessions relatively close together rather than spreading them throughout the day.

Performing the Mudra

This Mudra can be performed in either a seated or upright position. Settle your breathing and focus on this for a few minutes before performing the Mudra itself. Using both hands touch the tip of your ring finger and middle finger to the tip of your thumb, keeping your index and little fingers straight. Continue to focus on your breathing for a few minutes and then place your hands gently on your thighs, continuing to breathe deeply for the duration of the exercise.

Mudra 5: Chakra Mudra

Meaning and Health Benefits

"Chakra" is usually associated, in Western minds at least, with the concept of Chakras in general, in this context however, the true meaning of the word in translation ("wheel") applies. This Mudra has numerous health benefits and in terms of weight loss it is helpful in establishing healthy digestive processes, aiding in the uptake of important nutrients in the most natural way.

Effectiveness

The Mudra should be practiced for around 4five minutes but this can, again, be split into shorter sessions of no less than 1five minutes. This is a gentle, slow acting Mudra and should be performed regularly and over longer periods of time to ensure proper digestive function.

Performing the Mudra

Perform this Mudra in a seated position, ensuring you are relaxed and comfortable before beginning. Rest your left thumb on the right and interlace your fingers, extending your little fingers upwards until the tips touch lightly together. Place your hands in front of your navel and relax, focusing on your breathing until you have finished the exercise.

Mudra 6: Prana Mudra

Meaning and Health Benefits

Prana is the essential life force present in all things in the universe, and believed to emanate from the sun. This Mudra is about energy and strength, in both the physical and mental sense. It imparts a general feeling of health and energy, both of which promote activity and help with weight loss. In addition, it motivates and encourages us. This makes it a very useful Mudra if you are dieting, helping you to build your self-confidence.

Effectiveness

While the Prana Mudra helps you to lose weight through becoming more active the real benefit is in the sense of self-esteem that this Mudra develops. Motivating yourself to lose weight can be at least half of the battle and this Mudra raises your confidence, your energy levels and will be a useful Mudra to use long-term to maintain a healthier lifestyle. You can perform this Mudra for anything from 1five to 30 minutes and, for effective weight loss, you should consider performing it twice a day; first thing in the morning and again in the evening being the ideal times.

Performing the Mudra

Perform this Mudra with both hands and in a comfortable seated position. If, however, you are feeling low in terms of energy or mood the Mudra can be performed anywhere, in any position, for a fast acting energy boost. Place your hands on your thighs with the palms facing upwards and touch the tips of your thumb, little and ring finger, keeping your middle and index fingers straight.

Mudra 7: Surhabi Mudra

Meaning and Health Benefits

The "Cow" Mudra is an excellent Mudra for improving the digestive system and is also considered to be one of the most powerful Mudras. It combines the power of all of the elements and, in terms of weight loss, improves digestion, removes toxins and harnesses the nutrition of "good" food in the correct way. It provides relief from a whole range of stomach ailments and is considered excellent for combating indigestion. The Mudra also helps improve concentration and confidence.

Effectiveness

Extremely powerful, this Mudra brings all the forces of the universe to your aid. Performed twice a day, again, once in the morning and evening, is the recommended way in which to achieve the most positive results. The Mudra should be performed for 4five minutes per day but this can be broken down into five minutes per session as required.

Performing the Mudra

This is one of the most complex Mudras and can take a little practice to get right. Use the image above for reference and the following directions as a guide; bring the tip of your little finger together with the tip of your ring finger on the opposite hand and the tip of your index fingers to the tip of your middle fingers on the opposite hand. Finally touch the tips of your thumbs gently together.

Mudra 8: Adho Mukh Mudra

Meaning and Health Benefits

The "facing down" Mudra is one of the simpler Mudras to perform (a relief after the Surhabi Mudra) and is beneficial as it helps to activate healthy and rapid digestion processes. This is also a cleansing Mudra and will remove toxins and fats from the body making it a perfect all-round Mudra for weight loss.

Effectiveness

This is another strong and simple Mudra which will work rapidly. It should only be performed for short periods of time, no more than five minutes in one session. If you wish, you can perform the Mudra several times a day but no more than four times in a single day.

Performing the Mudra

The Mudra can be performed in a seated or standing position and thanks to its rapid workings can be performed at any time or location you choose. Bring your palms together with all of your fingers pointing downwards.

Mudra 9: Avahan Mudra

Meaning and Health Benefits

The Avahan Mudra is the "calling" Mudra and it brings assistance in the form of strength. The Mudra draws energy into the body and also helps the body to use energy efficiently. It aids the digestive system by promoting rapid but efficient digestion and assimilation of the food we consume. Again, as with several of the other Mudras, the Avahan Mudra also brings strength in the form of will-power which will help to both resit cravings and to diet effectively.

Effectiveness

The "strength" aspect of this Mudra helps your body to build the strength it needs by absorbing nutrients more efficiently. The willpower element is also useful and you may find that this Mudra encourages help in your efforts to lose weight, sometimes from unexpected sources. The Mudra appeals for assistance and it appeals to the divine, or to universal energy, for this assistance. The Mudra can be performed for 30 minutes, once a day, or for five minutes at a time several times a day.

Performing the Mudra

This gesture is one of supplication of asking for assistance, bring your palms towards your face, facing inwards, crossing your thumbs over them to lightly rest below your ring fingers. Allow your little fingers to touch each other along the sides and the edges of your palms to also touch.

Mudra 10: Manipur Chakra Mudra

Meaning and Health Benefits

This Mudra is related to the Solar Plexus Chakra and, as such, its direct health benefits include improved digestion. It is also linked to the ability to accept things in life and this is understood to mean in a physical, emotional or spiritual sense. The Mudra helps us to accept events around us, which in turn leads to a reduction in stress. Stress is linked to many health problems and can impact badly on the stomach and digestive system. By simply helping to reduce stress in life this Mudra helps our bodies to work more naturally.

Effectiveness

Considered highly effective for those looking to achieve balance and perspective in their lives it's also a great Mudra for those battling with weight loss. This Mudra can be used for up to 30 minutes at a time and can be used twice a day; it's a good idea to perform this Mudra once early in the morning and once again at the end of the day. This aids you in dealing with everything the day can throw at you and also in dismissing the events of the day (if they've been difficult) before you sleep!

Performing the Mudra

This Mudra can be performed in a standing position but is recommended to be performed sitting. Relax your body and breathe deeply; interlock all of your fingers and your thumbs, with the exception of your middle fingers which should remain pointing straight up. Place your hands in the area of your Solar Plexus Chakra and continue to breathe in and out deeply for the period you choose to use the Mudra.

Mudra 11: Shankh Mudra

Meaning and Health Benefits

The Shankh Mudra means "conch" and is related to respiratory function and to mental calm and balance. These traits are useful in weight loss in the same way as the previous

Mudra, creating a calm sensation which helps us to battle both stress and cravings. The Mudra is also linked to aiding digestive healing and this is, again, important for those who are dieting.

Effectiveness

This is a very effective, but gentle acting Mudra, which has a slow, subtly acting affect. You can practice this Mudra for 4five minutes, and as with many of the Mudras this time can be split into shorter sessions but for best effect split the time into no less than 1five minute slots.

Performing the Mudra

Perform this Mudra in a seated position with your back straight and keep your breathing calm and relax your body. Wrap all of the fingers of your right hand around the thumb of your left. Bring the tip of your right thumb to the tip of your middle finger of your left hand, keeping the other fingers of your left hand parallel with this middle finger. Bring your hands to rest just in front of your sternum (the breast bone).

Mudra 12: Vayu Mudra

Meaning and Health Benefits

The "Wind of God" Mudra relates to the element of air, in all its many incarnations. It's believed to help balance the air inside the body and is strongly related to health conditions including indigestion and flatulence. It helps while dieting, especially if you are training your body to eat new foods and it can also be used long term to ease other conditions including rheumatism, joint pain, arthritis and back pain.

Effectiveness

This is a highly effective Mudra and although you can use it frequently it's ideally used to deal with indigestion or flatulence as they occur. You can practice for as long as the problem persists or simply use every day for around 1five minutes to keep your body in a natural balance.

Performing the Mudra

The Mudra can be performed either sitting or standing, though standing is usually more effective. Press the tips of each index finger to the mound that lies just below your thumb and then fold your thumb to lightly press down onto the index finger, keeping your remaining fingers straight. As with the other Mudras described in this book, use both hands for the best effect.

Mudra 13: Kangula Mudra

Meaning and Health Benefits

Meaning "hidden potential", this Mudra is also known as the "plow" Mudra and is strongly related to new beginnings, growth and development. Physically, it can be understood to finding strength both physical and emotionally, helping you to use your own hidden abilities to achieve positive results. Related to growth, it is also about using nutrition within food to its best potential and is excellent and promoting healthy digestion.

Effectiveness

This is a good Mudra for long term use and can be used for up to 4five minutes at a time and is safe to use twice a day. Again, the time can be split into shorter spells and it can be a good Mudra to use several times a day, before and after meals.

Performing the Mudra

This Mudra can be performed either seated or standing and can be performed at any time and in any location. Press your ring finger into the center of your palm lightly and join the tips of your remaining fingers and thumb together so that they point upwards.

Mudra 14: Abhaya Hridaya Mudra

Meaning and Health Benefits

This Mudra means "courageous heart" and is related not just to bravery and developing an open, giving emotional personality but to the physical health of your heart. In relation to weight loss this is important, as a healthy heart makes for an all-round healthy body. As part of weight loss you will need to incorporate healthy exercise and this Mudra will help to strengthen your heart so that it is fully up to the challenge!

Effectiveness

A very effective Mudra that can be practiced from five to 4five minutes at a time. You can practice this Mudra twice a day and ideally practice for the same amount of time on each occasion.

Performing the Mudra

Perform this Mudra in a seated position. Bring your palms together facing each other and then cross the palms at the wrist with the right wrist closer to the body than the left. Interlock your middle, index and little fingers and join the tips of your ring finger and thumb together, placing your hands in the area of your heart. One of the more complex Mudras, this can take a little practice!

Mudra 15: Bharani Vaataayana Mudra

Meaning and Health Benefits

Meaning "precious horse" or "jewel amongst horses" this Mudra is said to balance the elements of earth, fire and water within our bodies. It gives us an "overview" perspective in life, allowing us to see the big picture. Not directly related to weight loss in a physical sense, this Mudra is best understood as being helpful at maintaining our motivation, in seeing the end result of our actions.

Effectiveness

Though not directly, or apparently, helping with weight loss the Mudra is very powerful at maintaining a positive outlook and at helping you to see the results of your actions. While dieting it can feel that you are getting nowhere fast but using the Mudra will enable you to see that in reality progress is occurring and help you to focus on your goal. You can perform the Mudra for 4five minutes at a time, or split this into five or 1five minute slots.

Performing the Mudra

One of the simpler Mudras to perform, this Mudra can be performed seated or standing. Join your hands together and interlace all of your fingers and the thumbs. Now extend the thumbs, the ring fingers and the little fingers outward, pressing them lightly together.

Chapter 4 - Curbing Cravings and Building Willpower

Anybody who has experienced one or more diets in their lives will happily tell you that the biggest problems they face are cravings and maintaining willpower. We've touched on both in the previous chapter and the Mudras described there but in this final chapter we'll take them head on! All of the Mudras described here address these issues and will be essential in your efforts to lose weight and to keep that weight off for good.

Mudra 16: Tritiiya Vayu Mudra

Meaning and Health Benefits

This is Mudra is based on the Vayu Mudra – the Wind of God – and in this case the effects are related to mental aspects of the element air. This is one of the most beneficial Mudras for beating cravings and will be extremely useful for those who have changed their diet or who have cut out certain food types. In this case the Mudra dispels negative thoughts and actions rapidly.

Effectiveness

This is a very strong Mudra and can be performed either in short bursts, as and when needed, or in longer sessions for up to 4five minutes and either once or twice a day. Often the best use of this Mudra is when cravings attack.

Performing the Mudra

The Mudra can be performed anywhere at any time and can be performed seated or standing. To form the Mudra place the tips of your thumbs on the mound below the ring fingers. Now bring the middle, ring and little fingers over the thumbs. Interlock the index fingers together holding the top phalange of each against the other. Hold the Mudra in front of your forehead to block, or blow away, negative thoughts and cravings.

Mudra 17: Prithvi Mudra

Meaning and Health Benefits

This is an Earth Mudra, strongly associated with grounding, with adapting to new routines and to establishing new habits. In terms of dieting, this will help you to adjust to new habits, in relation to eating and exercise habits. The Mudra helps to foster balance, self-confidence and creates balance within the whole body.

Effectiveness

This is profoundly calming and very effective Mudra. It's used in many contexts by many people, simply to achieve a sense of balance and in order to assist in helping projects grow and come to fruition. It can be performed at least twice a day for 30 to 4five minutes and can be performed in shorter bursts of at least five minutes.

Performing the Mudra

Perform this Mudra in a seated position. Place your palms in your lap, facing upward and touch the tips of your ring finger and thumb, pressing them together lightly. Keep your remaining fingers pointing outwards.

Mudra 18: Usha Mudra

Meaning and Health Benefits

This is the Mudra of the morning and brings alertness and vitality. It's useful for waking early in the morning and for bringing a high level of energy. In terms of general health and fitness this is the best Mudra to get you stimulated and active first thing in the morning which is good for both your health and making also useful if you are dieting. In addition it will bring energy and motivation for those who are becoming accustomed to a new exercise regime.

Effectiveness

This is one of the fastest acting and most effective Mudras; ideally it should be performed for no more than 10 minutes but five is usually more than enough. It's best to perform this Mudra when you first awake and face towards the east, where the sun rises. Many people find this Mudra more powerful than the strongest shot of caffeine!

Performing the Mudra

This is a very simple Mudra to perform. Simply relax and regulate your breathing. You can perform the Mudra in bed or in a seated position. Clasp your hands together, with the left thumb, index finger and so on, over the right – the Mudra can be likened to the gesture of prayer in many cultures.

Mudra 19: Vajra Mudra

Meaning and Health Benefits

The Mudra of lightening, this Mudra brings confidence, willpower and the ability to act keenly and decisively. This helps you to battle the psychological aspects of weight loss and brings firmness of action which will help you to rapidly achieve goals and plans.

Effectiveness

This is another fast acting and powerful Mudra. Use as and when required but for no less than five minutes at a time. You can use the Mudra for 4five minutes in one go or split into shorter sessions as required. It's an excellent Mudra for using before you set out for the day, helping you to deal with the day in a direct, focused and inspired way.

Performing the Mudra

Hold your hands in front of the area of your heart and wrap the index finger of one hand in the thumb and fingers of the other, with the remaining fingers of your hand curl the fingers to form another fist.

Mudra 20: Uttarabodhi Mudra

Meaning and Health Benefits

This is the Mudra of Enlightenment and it helps to bring a sense of peace, dispels fears and stress and brings strength and confidence to those who practice it. It brings will-power and the ability to face and overcome obstacles. It's used to dispel stage-fright or to combat exam nerves and is excellent for those striving to lose weight through both dieting and exercise, bringing the confident knowledge that you can achieve your goal.

Effectiveness

Perform this Mudra for short five minute bursts or longer sessions of up to 40 minutes. It's a fast acting and very powerful Mudra and can help to bring a boost to yourself confidence and beat cravings as well as simply get you through a difficult day.

Performing the Mudra

You can perform this Mudra seated, standing and in any location as required. Relax and breathe deeply, bringing your hands together with the palms facing each other. Interlace your fingers and then bring the tips of your index fingers together and the tips of your thumbs together. Extend the index fingers, still touching, upwards and the thumbs, still touching, downwards.

Developing a Routine

If you were to practice all of the Mudras described in this book you'll probably notice that it could take all day, assuming you perform each for the maximum time! In order to lose weight successfully, developing a routine is essential. This is true in all areas of your life including the use of Mudras. Remember that Mudras are gestures that focus intent; by regularly practicing them you not only bring the power of universal energy to your efforts but also the focused power of your own mind. Creating a routine reinforces this focus.

To use Mudras to lose weight you may find it easier to focus on the first three Mudras, described in Chapter 2 combined with those in this chapter, to aid in losing excess body weight in the early stages and to build the willpower that you will need for your efforts. You can concentrate on these Mudras for one, two, three or more weeks as required but, importantly, try to practice them for the maximum amount of time and to ensure that you stick to this practice rigidly, every day. It's also a good idea to try to ensure that you pick (and stick to) a specific time each day to practice your Mudras, as this is generally believed to make the more effective.

From this point on you can focus on the remaining Mudras described in Chapter 3, to help your body recover and adjust to your new regime. You may wish to continue using both the Mudras in Chapter 2 and this chapter but you can cut the time that you practice each. A good routine would be to take your favorite Mudra from Chapter 2 and practice this for five minutes before picking one from Chapter 1 to perform for longer periods, finally adding one from this Chapter to keep your confidence and craving combating abilities high!

Using this routine should help to ensure that you get the best from Mudras for weight loss. Having read the individual Mudras you can also tailor your routine to use Mudras that you believe will be most useful for you. For example, if cravings are your biggest enemy use Mudra 16 (the Tritiiya Vayu Mudra) on a daily basis for as long as necessary. You can also add many of the Mudras, as required, to combat specific issues on a short term basis and many can be used in any location, whether seated or standing. Again, as an example, incorporate Mudra 12 (the Vayu Mudra) if indigestion strikes!

Long Term Use of the Mudras

The Mudras described in this book are designed to help you lose weight and to also keep that weight off. For the most effective results in terms of remaining at a healthy weight it is advisable to maintain long term use of the Mudras, you may wish to reduce the time you spend on the practice of Mudras but once the habit is established, and you've seen for yourself the results, it's likely you'll be keen to continue with the practice. I hope that this book has given you enough information to begin using Mudras for weight loss and wish you the best of luck with your journey!

Conclusion

Thank you again for reading this book!

I hope this book was able to help you to learn the ancient technique of practicing the Mudras. Although some of these are easier than others I hope you will find that with time you are able to master them all!

The next step is to begin to learn the Mudras, one by one, and start practicing them every day. I hope that you soon begin to see the benefits and wish you the best of luck!

Finally, if you enjoyed this book, please take the time to share your thoughts and post a review on Amazon. It'd be greatly appreciated!

Thank you and good luck!

Printed in the USA
CPSIA information can be obtained
at www.ICGtesting.com
LVHW010812230923
758723LV00011B/4